I0139901

LIFE ON THE ROCK

ODIE JONES, JR.

PUBLISHER: STORYLINE PUBLISHING, L.L.C.

TAMPA, FLORIDA

LIFE ON THE ROCK/ODIE JONES, JR.

Library of Congress Control Number: 2017904916

ISBN: 978-0-9979373-1-2

Editor: Deidre R. Jones

Published by: Storyline Publishing, L.L.C.

Printed in the United States of America

Looking from the center of the photo, at 4-o'clock and at the base of Mt. Sivuqaq is Northeast Cape AFS. Directly left of the station is the White Alice Site. The radome is obscured by clouds atop Mt. Sivuqaq.

Alaska polar bear with her cubs

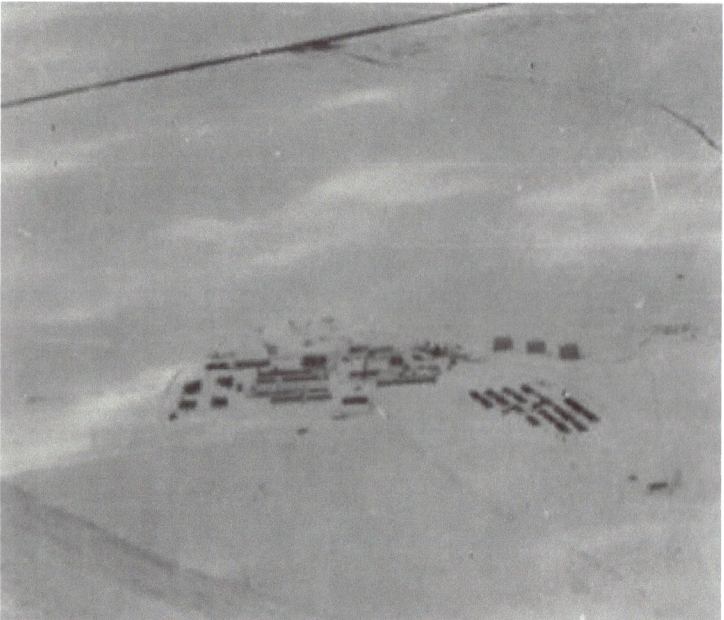

Snowbound Northeast Cape AFS, St. Lawrence Island, Alaska. The runway is in the background to the far north (Photo by N.E. Cape Photo Lab).

Intentionally Blank

CONTENTS

PROLOGUE

After I graduated from high school, there was so much pressure on me to hurry up and get started in life until I was in a whirlwind. I was poor and there was little time to think about what I was going to do because my choices were few and in between. I couldn't get decent work in the Town of Aliceville, in the County of Pickens, or the State of Alabama. To me, growing up on the farm and staying on the farm after graduation was like giving up. Twelve years of schooling had taught me that there was so much more in life than share-cropping.

We were on such a fast track that I changed her name from Dorothy to Dotty. Regardless of being settled financially with a decent job or not, life moved on. In my case, I felt the pressure of having to get married and start a family to call myself a grown man. We were very young but felt an urgency that marriage was our destiny. A little over one month after we wed, I enlisted into the Air Force (Dotty thought I was already enlisted and had plenty money). I still don't know how I did that. We didn't even have a home of our own when the *most beautiful baby in the world* came into our lives. We named her Sheila because we thought it meant *queen*. Dotty's parents decided that we were too immature to care for her so they took charge. In the meantime, Uncle Sam sent me off to the Rock (isolated N.E. Cape AFS, Alaska) for one year.

My dream of attending writers school had already been aborted by USAF Basic Military Training at Parks AFB, Pleasanton, California and Communications Center Specialist School at Warren AFB, Cheyenne, Wyoming. There was nothing to remind me that the Territory of Alaska existed, therefore it never occurred to me that I would end up there.

The reason for writing this story is simply to combine a little of my subjective experiences with some history of an important Air Force installation located in the remote tundra of Alaska. Aside from writing this story, I found time for writing letters home, composing poems, weight lifting, helping in the photo lab and singing tenor with a *doo wop* quintet sometimes called the "Capers,"

This story is meant to be historical, educational and entertaining. I hope you will enjoy reading it.

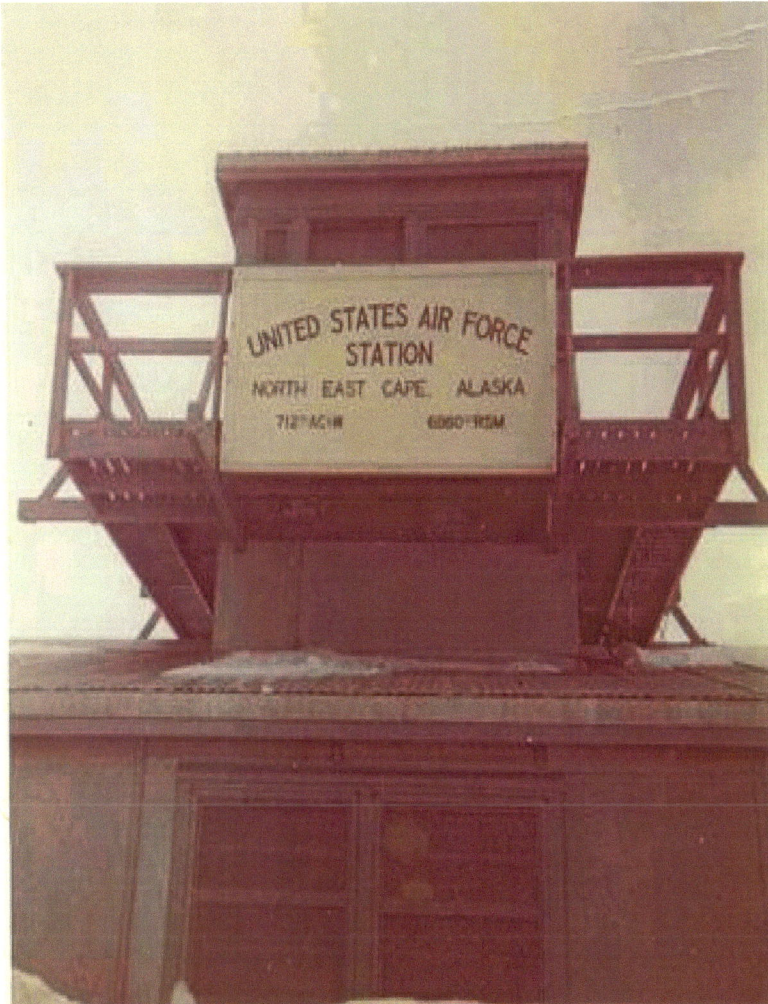

Northeast Cape Air Force Station Landmark

Northwest Cape   **Savoonga**   **Northeast Cape**

Southwest Cape   **Siknik Cape**   **Southeast Cape**

Map of St. Lawrence Island, Alaska

Alaska Male Walrus

LIFE ON THE ROCK/ODIE JONES, JR.

ACKNOWLEDGEMENTS

Alphonse Fernandez

Donald Campbell

Ebony Walker

Elijah Hall

George Ellis

Herman Baker

Iva Carter

Jim McCaa, Jr.

Josephine Hubbard

Karen Smith

Marvin Graham

Robert Allen

Tracy Jones

DEDICATIONS

To my mother, Mrs. Josephine Jackson – Madear, my love for you is eternal. You gave me life. I can't ask for anything more.

To my baby girl, Deidre, you are a smart daughter. Thanks for your outstanding knowledge and patience.

To my Jones family because I love all of you.

Alaska Caribou (Reindeer).

St. Lawrence Island, Alaska is shown in the lower left corner of the above map.

Note: Gambell, Alaska is 35 miles from Russia.

Mother and newborn baby moose.

CHAPTER 1 - ST. LAWRENCE ISLAND

Alaska was purchased from Russia in 1867 for $7,200,000. When Secretary of State William Seward agreed to a settlement and President Andrew Johnson signed the treaty, the sale ended Russia's presence in North America. Until gold was discovered, it was called, "Seward's Folly." Alaska remained a US Territory until 1959, when it became the 49th state of the USA.

There are reportedly 2,670 named islands in Alaska which enables it to be the largest state in the United States. The fourth largest island in Alaska is St. Lawrence Island which is 1,983 square miles. It is thought to be one of the last surviving non-submerged parts of a land bridge that once joined Asia (Chukotsk

LIFE ON THE ROCK/ODIE JONES, JR.

Peninsula of Siberia) with North America. It is thirty-seven miles east-southeast from the Siberian coastline, Union of Soviet Socialist Republic and one hundred sixty-two miles from Nome, the Alaskan Mainland.

The U.S. federal penitentiary at Alcatraz Island, San Francisco, California was America's premier maximum-security prison from 1934 until 1963. It was called the "Rock" perhaps because it was once the final stop for the nation's most incorrigible prisoners. Please do not confuse Alcatraz Island with St. Lawrence Island.

To the contrary, St. Lawrence Island is situated in the middle of the Bering Sea and no one there was imprisoned. This massive lump of volcanic rock is U.S. territory lovingly referred to as The Rock! The fact that it is called that is not the folly of a tourist agency; the island is composed of big rocks, little rocks, and more rocks.

A2C Jones: "Who me? Oh, I thought I could see Russia from up here." (Photo by Herman Baker)

Initially, it was difficult to believe that we were located so close to the Soviet Union. Ironically, on a sunny day, we sometimes boasted that we could see Russia with the *naked eye*. I am sure, however that someone else had previously laid claim to that allegation. There is also a saying that you will find *a beautiful woman behind every tree*. There were no trees to be found on The Rock -- Not even a bush. Notta!

About seeing Russia from Alaska, on September 15, 2008, Nina Rastogi, The Explainer, wrote an article entitled, "Can You

LIFE ON THE ROCK/ODIE JONES, JR.

Really See Russia From Alaska?" It stated: "In her Sept. 11 interview with ABC's Charlie Gibson, Sarah Palin had this to say about Russia: 'They're our next-door neighbors, and you can actually see Russia from land here in Alaska, from an island in Alaska.' 'Is that true?' 'Yes. Russia and Alaska are divided by the Bering Strait, which is about 55 miles at its narrowest point. In the middle of the Bering Strait are two small, sparsely populated islands: Big Diomede, which sits in Russian territory, and Little Diomede, which is part of the United States. At their closest, these two islands are a little less than two and a half miles apart, which means that, on a clear day, you can definitely see one from the other.' "The Diomede Islands are often blanketed by persistent fog, which makes visibility difficult. On a clear day, though a person standing at sea level can see a little less than three miles across the ocean. You can see farther if you go higher—at the highest altitude on Little Diomede (919 feet), you can see for about 37 miles...."

St. Lawrence Island is mountainous, with the highest rock being in the immediate area of 1,600 feet. The flat area close to the water was tundra which was soft and spongy during the summer and hard as a brick during the winter. Grass and flowers were seen; there were supposedly Texas Bluebonnets, and a local plant known as Alaskan Cotton.

Native grass, dubbed Alaskan Cotton, blooms in June and July (Photo by Verna E. Pratt)

Only the snow Cat (center background) can travel between quarters and operations buildings during winter months (Photo by N.E. Cape Photo Lab).

CHAPTER 2 - THE MISSION AND SITE

Under Eleventh Air Force, a radar system was set up to warn of Japanese attacks which stretched from Point Barrow to Shemya, however it was dismantled after the end of the war. With the outbreak of the Cold War, plans were made by Alaskan Air Command (AAC) to establish a new system for air defense. Discussions ensued and several plans were proposed and modified, until, in 1948 a plan was agreed on and funded by Congress in 1949 for ten radar sites for Alaska.

In the early 1950s, fear of Japanese attack gave way to fear of attack by the Soviet Union. The Soviets established numerous airfields in northern Siberia that represented the most significant threat of Soviet attack on North America. Planners had made their final site selections for a permanent Aircraft Control and Warning System. Five early-warning surveillance sites were located on the western Alaskan coast: Cape Lisbourne AFS; Cape Newenham AFS; Cape Romanzof AFS; Tin City AFS and Northeast Cape AFS.

Northeast Cape Air Force Station was a forward outpost, located on St. Lawrence Island in the Bering Sea, between Alaska and Siberia. The base was a continental defense radar station constructed to provide the United States Air Force early-warning of an attack by the Soviet Union on Alaska. The station was the closest forward radar surveillance station to mainland Soviet Union.

The opening of Northeast Cape AFS was done by a combination of Air Force visionaries and real pioneers of the arctic north. From the very first site survey the men seemingly faced problems of *insurmountable* proportions but they endured. The improvements in the surveillance mission justified overcoming the problems encountered during the move.

Communications were initially provided by a high frequency radio system which proved unreliable because of atmospheric disturbances in the high latitudes. After investigating various options, AAC decided to build a system of Air Force-owned tropospheric scatter transmitters that bounced radio signals off the Troposphere, and microwave radio relay sites over short ranges of about 50 miles.

By the late 1950s, Alaska's air defense infrastructure was well developed in scope and depths, providing early warning and interception for the territory itself, for the United States, and for North America. Fear of Soviet air attack gave way to fear of Soviet missile attack. America constructed the Ballistic Missile Early Warning system (BMEWS) and the Distant Early Warning (DEW) stations across Alaska and Canada. The AC&W stations, the DEW lines and BMEWS were linked together by the White Alice (Alaska Integrated Communications and Electronics) system. This provided a revolutionary and reliable multi-channel communications system for all-weather atmospheric conditions. Several air bases were constructed to support these systems. As with Northeast Cape AFS, each site was a self-contained outpost, with housing for personnel and an airstrip for occasional delivery of supplies and personnel.

The site was located on approximately 4,800 acres of land at the base of the small Mount Sivuqaq along the northeast coast of St. Lawrence Island. It was constructed so that an individual could go from any one place to another without exposing himself to the outside. There were about 25 buildings and extra support structures; all connected by covered and heated corridors. The story goes that some personnel never went outside during their whole tour on the island. It's possible, but very unlikely, especially for Detachment personnel. Our working area was located approximately one- half mile from the quarters; in the operations building. We worked 12-hour shifts and traveled back and forth in a snowmobile called the "weasel" during severe weather.

The 712th AC&W Sqdn personnel operated AN/FPS-3 and AN/FPS-20A radars. As a surveillance station, its mission was to monitor the airspace for aircraft activity and provide information 24/7 to the Air Defense Direction Center at Murphy Dome AFS near Fairbanks, AK. The information was analyzed to determine range, direction, altitude, speed and whether aircraft were friendly

or hostile.

An airman monitors the radar scope.

The radome located atop Mount Sivuqaq at Northeast Cape AFS, Alaska.

LIFE ON THE ROCK/ODIE JONES, JR.

Det. 1, 6981st RGM's Morse Code intercept operators and linguists trained in the Russian language were tasked with the surveillance and collection of voice and electronic signals, to be forwarded to the National Security Agency for intelligence analysis. A direction-finding receiver was also manned, both for surveillance and search and rescue. Teletypewriter operators manned the telecommunications center to send and receive printed hard-copy messages.

Teletypewriter Model 28 ASR Machine

They also operated Teletypewriter Model 28 ASR machines using 5-level paper tape perforators and readers at 60-words per minute. Incoming classified messages were decrypted and outgoing classified messages were encrypted by cryptographers for transmission.

The two trucks and the "weasel" (snowmobile) help to make up the motor pool. (Photo by N.E. Cape Photo Lab)

The tramway was used by maintenance personnel to travel to
and from the radome atop Mount Sivuqaq
(Photo by N.E. Cape Photo Lab).

CHAPTER 3 - PERSONNEL AND QUARTERS

It seems I was primed for my assignment on the Rock without knowing it. Maybe the Air Force didn't calculate it with the Rock in mind, but it sure turned out looking like it was in the program. I was sent to Francis E. Warren AFB, Cheyenne, Wyoming where the weather was comparable to St. Lawrence Island at times. It was snowy and the temperatures dropped down below freezing in winter. Incidentally, during the school term, I was assigned to "fire guard" where I just happened to receive lots of survival experience in inclement weather.

After graduation from teletype school at Warren AFB in August 1956, I was ordered to report to Detachment 1, 6981st Radio Squadron Mobile (RSM), Northeast Cape AFS, Alaska.

LIFE ON THE ROCK/ODIE JONES, JR.

This was a United States Air Force Security Service (USAFSS) unit. There was a reorganization of the unit in September 1956 and Det. 1, 6981st RSM became Det. 1, 6981st Radio Group Mobile (RGM). To get there, I had to go to Elmendorf AFB, Anchorage, Alaska for a long flight out to St. Lawrence Island. I viewed the Air Force's inventory of cargo aircraft to be modern and passenger friendly. My flying experience was limited so I was oblivious to the older airplanes still in the inventory.

An AC-47 Skytrain ("Goony Bird") aircraft on the runway
at
Northeast Cape AFS, Alaska

LIFE ON THE ROCK/ODIE JONES, JR.

So, to my dismay, I was hauled to my first duty station in a C-47 Skytrain which was lovingly referred to as the "Goony Bird." I say *hauled* because the flight across the Bering Sea seemed like riding in a wagon during Death Valley Days. At times, I was sure I felt a draft of wind coming through the side of the plane and I could almost touch the waves outside. Luckily, I had plenty time to recuperate from the bumpy flight because my tour of duty on The Rock was one year from the date I arrived.

In addition to the Detachment, there was the 712th Air Control and Warning Squadron (712 AC&W Sqdn), Alaska Air Command (AAC). We were tenants on their installation at Northeast Cape. This meant that they provided us with transportation and logistic support, i.e., housing, messing, medical attention, etc. Although there were two different units on the Rock, we all got along like one big team. Also, occasionally there were a few Eskimo men who camped near the runway. With the construction of the site in 1952, many displaced islanders joined the Alaska National Guard to continue to provide land-based defense.

LIFE ON THE ROCK/ODIE JONES, JR.

As to living quarters, the lower airmen's barracks were two-man rooms, approximately eleven by fourteen feet. They were furnished with medium metal Hollywood-type beds. Also, metal desk-table combinations and chairs.

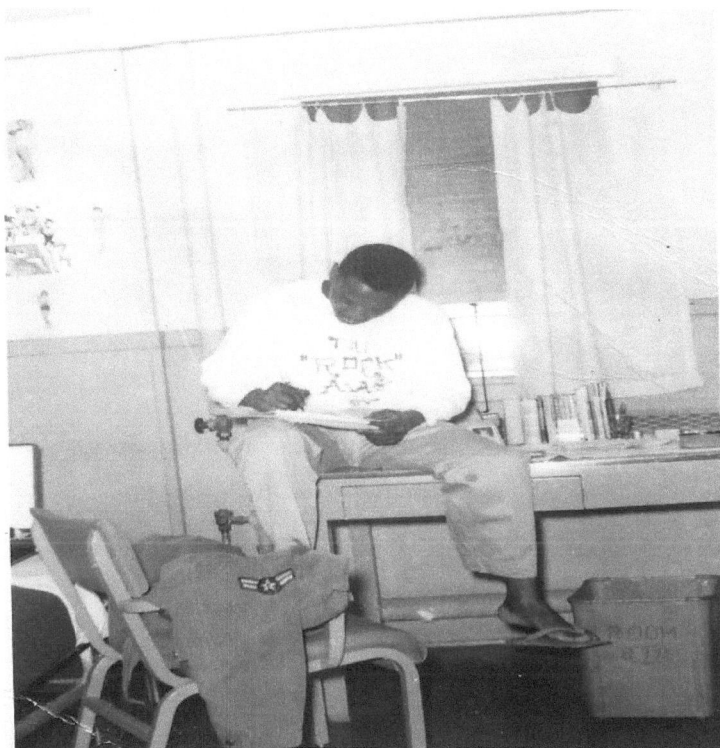

A2C Jones is catching up on some letter writing while his roommate is out. (Photo by Herman Baker)

Each room had linoleum floor covering and at least one window to allow comfortable ventilation. If the airman so desired, he could decorate his room by adding curtains. draperies, or throw rugs of his choosing. Each room had either one very large or two private closets with sufficient room for both the normal military issue and civilian clothes. The rooms were decorated in pastel colors and were equipped with individually controlled steam heat.

N.E. Cape living quarters (Photo by N.E. Cape Photo Lab).

CHAPTER 4 – FOOD AND SUPPLIES

To show the importance of forces being well-provisioned, Napoleon (19th century) once said, "An army marches on its stomach." As a consequence, his soldiers wrote "bogus" requisitions or marauded the local populace for food. Other times, they ate horse meat or committed suicide from hunger.

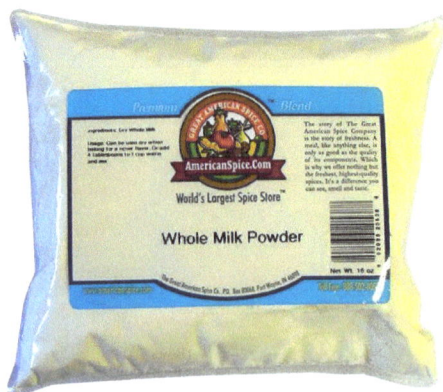

The Mess Hall (dining facilities) and chow (food) were pretty good at Northeast Cape AFS, considering the Rock was a remote military installation. Our milk came to us in a powdered form. Unlike Stateside, we did not have cows, as such, but we did have a *mechanical cow*. To reconstitute, the secret was in the re-combining formula. Our eggs arrived in dehydrated form too. But like the milk, we knew how to fix them up. The mess hall usually served four meals a day, except Sundays and holidays; when we had a lazy man's breakfast. It started at 0730 hours and continued until 1230 hours. The early birds could get two breakfasts if they desired.

LIFE ON THE ROCK/ODIE JONES, JR.

In the cartoon, Garfield said, "Avoid fruits and nuts. You are what you eat.," –Jim Davis.

In 1953, the Alaskan Air Command requested and received a special code named "Mona Lisa" for the program of delivering supplies. Supplies had to be shipped via air or water because roads and rail lines were either inadequate or, in most cases, nonexistent. A port was built on the Bering Sea so that the supply ship or barge could dock. The Air Force procured supplies and oversaw their loading onto Navy barges; the Navy (Military Sea Transport Service) carried the cargoes to the sites; the Army loaded them onto smaller barges and transported them to the beach; and finally, on-site Air Force personnel unloaded the cargoes and transported them to storage areas. The supplies also included construction equipment, vehicles and bulk materiel. This very important resupply mission was a once-a-year operation during the summer months because the waterways became all frozen over in winter.

A "Mona Lisa" resupply barge waiting at the docks
(Photo by 11th AF History Office Archives).

A2C Jones and A3C Graham relax after storing supplies during "Mona Lisa." (Photo by N.E. Cape Photo Lab)

Alaska salmon swimming upstream.

CHAPTER 5 - ENTERTAINMENT, RECREATION

AND SOCIAL LIFE

Movies were shown regularly, except on Mondays and Fridays; in a fairly modern theater. The theater had recently been provided equipment for the showing of Cinemascope pictures. The admission was 25 cents and there were two shows nightly, plus a matinee. Like everything else, the movie films came in by plane and when there was severe weather, they were delayed. Which meant that we had no movies until the plane came in. Occasionally, Special Services would organize a talent show to fill the gap. Singing, dancing and playing a musical instrument seemed to be the pastime of most local talent.

LIFE ON THE ROCK/ODIE JONES, JR.

DRIVE-IN CLOSED NIGHT AND DAY!

Occasionally, Special Services would organize a talent show to fill the gap. Singing, dancing and playing a musical instrument seemed to be the pastime of most local talent. After having two or three beers, a *wannabe* comedian might get up enough nerves to face the Rock audience. The Capers, (sometimes called the Harp tones or Flamingos), a local singing quintet was invited to perform in the USAF Talent Show at Elmendorf AFB in Anchorage. The commander of the 712 AC&W Sqdn said two of the men could go. The other three men were assigned to Det. 1, 6981st RGM (USAFSS) and due to their jobs being "mission essential," they weren't allowed to leave the island.

The Capers (above) were local singers of N.E. Cape AFS, Alaska. (Photo by N.E. Cape Photo Lab).

The recreation hall, located adjacent to the Base Exchange (BX) and theater, had ping-pong tables, pool tables, and shuffleboard, in addition to smaller games such as darts, checkers, etc. There was a good-sized day room provided with lounge chairs, tables, lamps, and a variety of magazines.

Weightlifting just wasn't for everybody.

A small room was used for those musclemen who wished to exercise with weights. There was a young man who lifted weights meticulously and he developed the muscles to prove it. I lifted them just enough to feel good and look better because somebody told me if you build the muscles and stop lifting the weight, you will blow up like a balloon. I was also told that is what happened to guys who ate a lot of potato chips and drank a lot of beer.

In as much as the whole Rock was a game preserve, there was no hunting. Personnel could fish in either the sea or any of the several small streams. Fishing equipment was available for purchase at the BX or loaned from Special Services.

Be careful of the crack in the ice.

As a result of the abundance of snow and because we lived at the foot of Mount Sivuqaq, one might think of it as a good location for skiing. It was, especially when the mountain was thoroughly covered with snow. Because of the importance of the mission, the prevailing hazards of skiing and the inherent liability placed upon the government installation, skiing was forbidden. In the hard of winter and during stormy season, one would be foolish to attempt it. However, we were all young American airmen; daring and determined not to be outdone.

Sliding down the mountainside on cardboard!

When the snowstorms subsided and the snow began to melt, a few of us walked up the side of the mountain for about 15 to 20 yards. We would tie pieces of cardboard or our field jackets to our mid-sections for seats. We slid down the steep and slippery slope, yelling all the way. Mind you, it didn't happen very often.

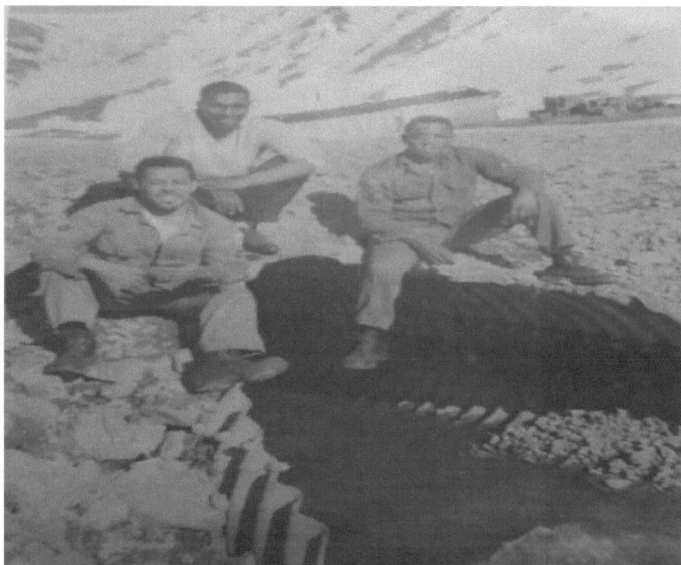

A2C Fernandez, A1C Ellis and A2C Jones
"hanging out" while off-duty

Social life off The Rock was non-existent. There were no towns or villages to visit; therefore, clubs were established on the station. There was an airmen's club, NCO club, and an officer's lounge. Membership for airmen was free; they merely paid for what they wanted. The NCO club membership fee was $2.00 per month. I don't know but the officers probably paid no more than $5.00 a month.

LIFE ON THE ROCK/ODIE JONES, JR.

A water cooler was located just inside of the Mess Hall and a dispenser filled with saltpeter (potassium nitrate) was also prominently positioned. The instructions said to take 1 tablet daily and drink plenty water to stay hydrated and prevent muscular cramps. The *word* among the troops was the saltpeter was given to suppress the sexual urges of us young men. Some said saltpeter was being added to the powdered eggs which caused them to turn a light green. Military authority denies these allegations.

The Rock had a well-stocked BX. It carried most normal necessities, such as shaving articles, soap, towels, tobacco products, etc. It also had a fine selection of hobby materials, including photographic equipment of good quality. One of the better attractions the BX had to offer was its fine selection of hand carved ivory items made by the Eskimos.

Walrus Antlers Ivory

Walrus Teeth and Ivory

Hand carved ivory

I have been unable to find much documentation of subjective experiences on the Rock during the period when I was there. In "Freedom Through Vigilance – History of USAFSS, 2012" Author Larry Tart merely touched the surface of the subject in a discussion with William "Sparky" Rogers in 2007. I will quote (in part) Mr. Roger's statement from the book: "I was assigned to Northeast Cape (St. Lawrence Island) from May '56 until April '57. At that time, we belonged to Det. 1, 6981st RGM – also known as the *3rd Herd.* " …" I had a collection of ivory carvings I got by trading C-rations with the natives, who came over to our area from Gambell. They were part of the Alaska National Guard and could use our BX and theatre. They also took us on dogsled rides in exchange for the rations'" …" We were collocated with an

AC&W site, and they always thought we were spying on them. We had a wire from our Ops to theirs so we could hear what they were tracking for comparison."

I found the above account by Mr. Rogers to be very enlightening and interesting. I wish I had the opportunity to have met him while I was there. Maybe I did and don't remember.

The names of the men that I can remember being on the Rock with me are: *Alphonse Fernandez, Donald Campbell, George Ellis, Herman Baker, Marvin Graham and Robert Allen.*

Alaska seal

CHAPTER 6 -TELEPHONE, NEWSCASTS, MUSIC
AND LIBRARY

In 1876, Alexander Graham Bell spoke into the mouthpiece of the telephone, "Mr. Watson, come here, I want to see you!" But it wasn't until 1892 that American Telephone and Telegraph (AT&T) opened a long-distance telephone line.

The TP-6 Telephone

The cellular phone was created in 1973 but it wasn't put on the market. until the 1980s.

LIFE ON THE ROCK/ODIE JONES, JR.

In 1956, we had an amateur radio station on The Rock. It was supplied with pretty good equipment and was operated by volunteers. We could talk to most places in the States and had regular schedules with HAMS (Hyman, Almay & Murray) or amateur radio operators who provided our personnel with telephone patches in order that we could talk directly to someone back home. It sure was wonderful to hear our loved ones at the other end!

For newscasts and music programs, we had an AFRS (Armed Forces Radio Station). It was connected directly to the States for

The Armed Forces
Radio Service

hourly news broadcasts and other important programs such as elections, baseball, basketball, football, hockey, boxing and other sporting events for those who were interested.

It also provided local disc jockey (DJ) programs where individuals could request the recordings they liked best. Local talent could be tape recorded and presented as the DJ so chose. The station operated approximately 18 hours daily.

We had a good library, with approximately 3000 books to select from. There were also a good many paper-bound books that arrived monthly. The library was open during the day for those personnel on shift work who desired to utilize the facilities. With nothing much going on, one could find reading quite soothing at times. I found it very stimulating as a *would-be-writer.*

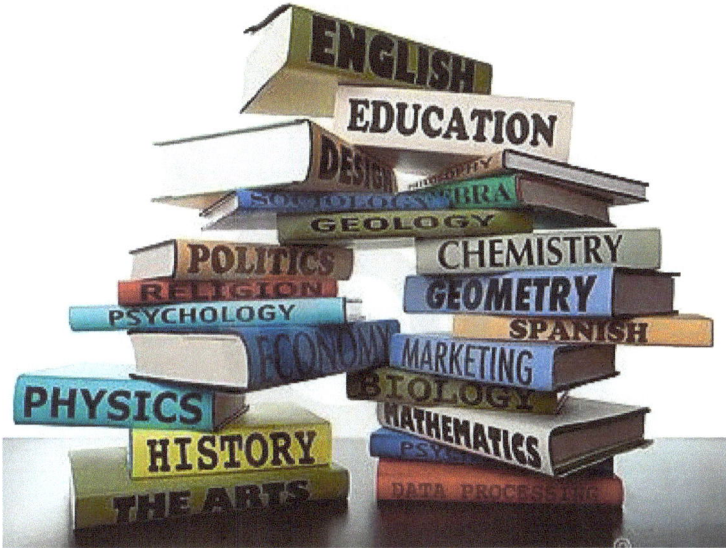

CHAPTER 7 - RELIGION, MEDICAL, PAY AND MAIL

Religious services were held most Sundays in the chapel. We did not have a regular chaplain, but services were held for both Protestant and Catholic volunteers.

Approximately once a month the organization was visited by "traveling" Chaplains of both faiths. A site choir was organized for those who liked to sing and could.

Personnel were constantly reminded of their responsibility for safety practices by themselves and their fellow airmen. They were charged to correct any unsafe act on the spot or report it to proper authorities as soon as possible.

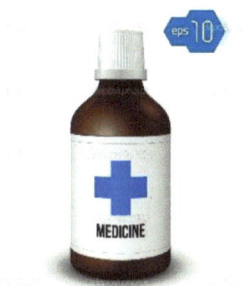

There was no doctor assigned to The Rock; however, two medics (medical technicians) were available at all times to cope with any medical problems. Serious cases were evacuated to Ladd AFB, Fairbanks, AK for necessary attention.

One thing other than rotation that was paramount in everyone's mind was payday. Unlike stateside or "Banana Belt" (Elmendorf Area), we were paid but once a month; the last day of each month!

Pay was in cash. Of course, there was nothing much to spend it on there. In case you are wondering, in 1956 we received overseas special pay since Alaska was a territory and not a state.

And now to the mail situation. Well, naturally it was not the same as it was stateside. All of our mail was brought in by aircraft, which was subject to delay due to adverse weather.

However, we did look forward to at least one mail delivery a week. One thing for sure, when it did come in, we had a lot of mail! The post office had facilities for sending and cashing money orders.

Included in the mail were packages from home. Whenever one of the guys got a *care package*, as we called it, the word went out and there was a reunion in that person's room. My mom was good at cooking anything but her caramel cakes would make your mouth water. It was in July, my birthday month, when I got my *care package*. The box seemed a little crushed from the long trip from Alabama but we never imagined someone had also kicked it around like a football. The fellows reminded me to thank my mom for the caramel *crumb* cake because it sure tasted good.

We were never sure if some of the packages didn't arrive on a *slow boat to Alaska* but we were still happy to get them. Another one of the guys received his care package from home which contained some homemade hog head cheese. By the time he was able to open the box, it seemed a little *ripe* but we enjoyed eating it with saltine crackers and washing it down with beer.

Regardless of the condition the care packages were in when they came in, they were well received because it was the thought that counted.

Care Package from home?

CHAPTER 8 - THE WEATHER AND CLOTHING

It would be a total misconception to think of Northeast Cape as having been an American resort like Florida or California. In that sense, it was not even in line with mainland Alaska. The weather became extremely rough at times. In summer: July and August, the maximum temperature was about 60 degrees, and fairly pleasant. The sun shone brightly, so you could get out and hike, play ball, fish, or participate in other outdoor activities. Winter started rolling around September or October with frosty weather and rain. From October through May, you could expect snow, high winds, and temperatures down to at least 35 degrees below zero. When it came to snow drifts being as high as buildings, Minot, North Dakota had nothing on the weather on the Rock.

The Radome is seen atop Mt. Sivuqaq, almost in the clouds.

Getting a little sun outside of the snow-covered radome.

Winter snow drifts at the N.E. Cape AFS quarters.

I was told that the temperature once dropped to 60 degrees below zero away from the buildings. The winds of Northeast Cape were the talk of Alaska; strong and gusty! During the frequent snow storms in winter, it was never safe to be outside alone. USAFSS recognized N. E. Cape AFS as having the most severe winters of all the command's worldwide permanent sites. At times, it was difficult to see your hand one foot in front of your face. If you spit, it became an icicle before it hit the ground.

LIFE ON THE ROCK/ODIE JONES, JR.

During my tour of duty, the maximum clocked winds at the airstrip was 94 knots (108.173 MPH). Stateside hurricanes had nothing on The Rock.

SSgt Campbell wearing the arctic parka.
(Photo by N.E. Cape Photo Lab)

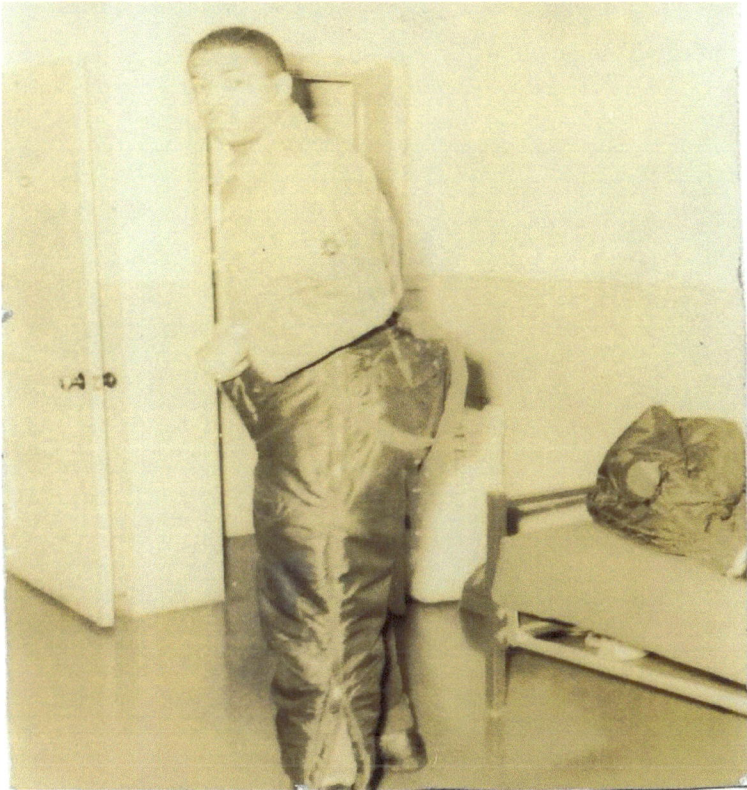

A2C Allen dressing in arctic clothing before work
(Photo by N.E. Cape Photo Lab).

Because of the bad weather, we were provided the best type of arctic clothing. This special clothing included a heavy lined parka equipped with a hood capable of covering the entire head and lower face. Special trousers of the same material were also issued. We received bunny boots, so named because of the white material used for their construction, shoe pacs and of course the old

61

overshoe. Wearing any one of these would keep you comfortable in freezing temperatures.

Bunny Boots

Arctic Mittens

As this painting depicts, it was never safe to be outside alone during a winter snow and wind storm.

To follow military regulations, personnel were expected to arrive on The Rock with their full issue of uniforms and some civilian clothing to lounge in. The uniform of the day was usually fatigues. Summer sun-tans or khakis were permitted but mixing of the uniforms was not allowed. The Rock was a military installation; therefore, the class "A" was a requirement to have available.

Laundry and cleaning facilities were in place. The site had a small laundry which was operated during off-duty hours by airmen qualified for such work. Of course, there was a slight charge; but for those who preferred to do their own, washers and dryers were provided in each bay.

Despite inclement weather outside, portable drying racks were unnecessary.

CHAPTER 9 - CUSTOMS AND COURTESIES

As previously stated, Northeast Cape AFS, The Rock was an official military installation; therefore, everyone was required to abide by military regulations. Personnel were expected to be clean and neat always. Periodic inspections were held of both personnel and quarters. The morale of personnel on the Rock depended on everyone striving jointly to make the station the best in the Air Force.

Despite close quarters, the salute was rendered when practical.

A3C Graham and A2C Jones pose after M-1 Carbine Rifle practice (Photo by N.E. Cape Photo Lab).

Just as with stateside bases, personnel at Northeast Cape were required to stay current in weapons training; in our case, it was with the M-1 Carbine Rifle.

There were no personnel leaves granted from the site except for emergencies, which were verified by the American Red Cross. Headquarters USAF was the approving authority for emergency leaves.

LIFE ON THE ROCK/ODIE JONES, JR.

Please keep in mind that The Rock was a remote site located in the Territory of Alaska which provided little of the amenities enjoyed by personnel stateside. Tours at the station were limited to one year because of the psychological strain and physical hardships. However, the job was an important one and we were proud to be able to serve our country in any manner required to insure the safety of our loved ones at home.

"Sorry, I can't talk any longer, must get packed because I'm rotating out on the next Iditarod sled."

Iditarod Dog Sled Race

ANIMAL NOTE – *During my tour of duty at Northeast Cape Air Force Station I never saw any of the animals pictured in this book.*

EPILOGUE

When thinking about keeping the Northeast Cape AFS operational, one must view it as a small town. The average Air Force base is maintained in much the same manner. One exception is the N.E. Cape was isolated from mainland Alaska. To some extent, it was independent, at least for a year at a time. The Annual Mona Lisa resupply had to be well calculated in order to sustain between missions. The thousands of professional personnel had to be thoroughly trained before arrival to *keep the lights shining* so to speak. On an average Air Force base, as well as in a small city, a runner can be dispatched to *borrow a cup of flour*. On the Rock, you had to depend upon each other because there were no neighbors to *call on for a flashlight*.

We already named MARS (Military Auxiliary Radio System), radar, radio, crypto, and communications center operators. Each of these specialists required maintenance personnel. Without mentioning managers and supervisors, additional occupations include, cook, supply, power production, vehicle maintenance, mail clerk, telephone, heavy equipment, weather, medic, tramway operator, fire chief, water specialist, waste management, and maybe others that I missed.

One of the greatest complications to operating a remote community like N.E. Cape is stocking ample spare-parts. Just about everything could be adjusted, re-arranged, by-passed, omitted or eliminated, if need be; except mission essential replacement parts. The second biggest obstacle was the inclement weather. The weather affected everything, including equipment and people's health and mental state. It was very expensive to maintain the Northeast Cape Air Force Station year in and year out.

LIFE ON THE ROCK/ODIE JONES, JR.

The above photo shows N.E. Cape AFS, St. Lawrence, Island, AK in 2003 after deactivation and prior to remediation. The White Alice communications array are at the base of the mountain. The radome is shrouded in clouds atop the mountain behind the White Alice site.

Throughout American history, technological advancements have caused the old to give way for the new. With the development of the satellite, advancements in communications, surveillance and overall defense measures have sped ahead by leaps and bounds. Because of these advancements and because of a reduction in the budget, the Rock was closed on September 30, 1969. The mission was assumed by other Alaskan Air Command surveillance radar sites with upgraded and more advanced equipment. After the station's deactivation, the communications antennas, radars, buildings and other structures sat neglected for over three decades. During those years of abandonment, property at the site had lost any value it had when the station was terminated. Eventually, in 2003 most of the structures were extracted in a very costly $10.5 million cleanup program. The remediation of the radar, support and White Alice communication station was completed by the 611th Civil Engineering Squadron, Elmendorf AFB, AK in 2005.

American bison (buffalo) and calf

"Well, good luck Jones and I won't tell on you!"

Intentionally Blank

LIFE ON THE ROCK/ODIE JONES, JR.

ABOUT THE AUTHOR

ODIE JONES, JR. is a native of Aliceville, Alabama. He is a graduate of Summerville High School, Aliceville, AL where he also earned the honor of Class Salutatorian. Jones retired from the U.S. Air Force June 1, 1984 after serving for twenty-eight years and attaining the rank of Senior Master Sergeant. He had numerous military assignments both in the U.S. and overseas; including one year in the Vietnam War. He received twenty-one prestigious awards and medals during his career. He is listed in the 2012 AF Memorial Registry and received the 2012 Airman's Society Certificate of Recognition.

As a charter member of the Bay Area Brotherhood, a nonprofit veteran's civic organization in Tampa, Florida. Jones has held the office of Treasurer, Secretary, Vice President and President multiple terms. He is the club's historian and primary writer. He is a life member of the Joint Communications Support Element Veterans Association and Vice President of the Gandy Civic Association, both in Tampa, FL. He briefly attended the University of Tampa, Tampa, FL.

LIFE ON THE ROCK/ODIE JONES, JR.

Odie has written numerous articles for military command publications and news releases for commercial newspapers. His most recently published book is "Saving the Lake at Bobby Hicks Park."

BIBLIOGRAPHY

Alaska's Animals, Alaska Department of Fish and Game.

Defending Attack from the North, Argonne National Laboratory for Environmental Planning (Cultural Resources) 611th Civil Engineer Squadron, PACAF, USAF.

Eleventh Air Force History Office Archives.

Freedom Through Vigilance, History of USAFSS, Vol. III, Larry Tart, 2012

Moved to N.E. Cape AFS, Landmark, Wade H. Ketron, '57

Northeast Cape Air Force Station – Wikipedia, the free encyclopedia.

Photos of N.E. Cape AFS, AK, Green Border.

Snopes – Barbara "hard truth" Mikkelson

Telephone TP-6 Western Electric 302AW contributed by Steve Cichossky (10/21/14)

Teletypewriter Model 28 ASR Copying ITTY – Museum of Communications – Seattle (Jun 3, 2009)

The Coldest Front – Office of History and Archaeology, Alaska Department of Natural Resources, Anchorage, AK

The Explainer, Nina Rastogi, "Can you really see Russia from Alaska?" (9/15/2008)

The Office of Website Management, Bureau of Public Affairs, US Department of State

Intentionally Blank

www.ingramcontent.com/pod-product-compliance
Lightning Source LLC
Chambersburg PA
CBHW040035110426
42741CB00031B/103